Breaking Through the Shackles

by

Joseph Somers

First published by Dog Ear Publishing
4010 W. 86th Street, Ste H
Indianapolis, IN 46268
www.dogearpublishing.net

ISBN: 978-159858-641-1

This book is printed on acid-free paper.

Printed in the United States of America

Preface

Life rolls back its curtain and showers challenges of every sort. Its claws of poverty can wrap you in the blanket of rejection, disappointment and shame. Ever been into the bottom-less pit of nothingness and feel like all hope is gone? You turn to the ones who should be there for you but you are slapped with rejection, baffled with the ugliness and baldness of life's unpleasant circumstances. Sometimes no matter how hard you try, hope seems to dance in the distant future, the place that lingers in the years tomorrow. My life has been the platform on which the chains of poverty have been manufactured. I have been tossed in the bowl of misfortune, suffering and pain, like a salad has been tossed in a dish ready to be devoured. At times I question even my very existence. Was it because I was the son of a heartless abuser, the seed of failing father? And to top it off, there was no love, from the outside world; it was just my mother and me. I reflected on the perfect man who came into this world, innocently, with nothing but good intentions. It happened to Him, He was rejected of men, abused and poverty stricken, but now He lives in a mansion, a home that He is preparing for me. I realize that God Himself gives us the test of time to prepare us as jewels for His kingdom.

I was determined to brace myself for the voyage, the path that He charted for me. I was determined to break through the disenchantment of the haves who lord themselves over the have-nots. Can you stand the test of your time? When you are thrown in life's sea of turmoil, will you make it? Well I did, and that is why I want to share my story with you. I want to show you that God never gives up on us even when our own reject us. The challenges that we face in life may just be the outer skin to be chiseled and sanded with the experience of life. The process is to reveal the spotless character that God intends for us to use to illuminate the lives of those we come in contact with. He did that for me. He can use you to make a difference in someone else's life, despite the binding shackles that are fused with life's calamity. My biological father proved to the world that he did not care, but my heavenly father showed unconditional love when He broke through the shackles of my life and gave me peace and contentment. His love far exceeds and transcends the curse by the progeny of my biological father. He gave me the strength to break through the physical challenge that was intended to retard my intellectual growth, the educational disability that charred my mental faculty, the poverty stricken life, that devoured my dignity. He gave me the will power and spiritual tenacity to break through the shackles and become a giant despite my stature.

I must share my story because He has given me gumption to stand like a giant and proclaim His power of deliverance. I am the son of a king, destined to live a life of prosperity. Now I realize that God can break through the shackles of contempt, shame and poverty. I was determined to prove to the world that a man must not be judged by the place where he was born or the parents to whom he was given but that a man was created in the image of God which unconditionally makes all men equal, regardless of color race, creed, wealth or poverty. It is not how you were born, or where you were born but the path that you take after you are born. It is God's intention for us to inhabit the earth, to prosper and occupy until He comes. He can tear down any barrier that blocks your path to success. He did just that for me. You can break through the shackles that spread its canopy of claim around you.

.

****

Chapter I

Held by the Shackles

Like a caged bird held in captivity, so was the beginning of my life, wrapped and entangled in a web of perpetual flames. I am a son of the soil, a native Jamaican, born in the little town of Port Antonio in the parish of Portland. I was the only child of my parents, and anticipated a life of love and happiness, but my dreams became the reality of a nightmare. My world started to crumble right before my very eyes and the chains of poverty imprinted its seal on the path of my life. I was held by the shackles of fear, suffering and pain. My hope was completely deflated, but my life was established upon the godly example and prayer of my beloved mother, Rosetta. I believe it is the dream of every boy to hold his father as a role model, a hero, someone to look up to and proudly say, "There goes my dad", but I could not.

At the age of three, the shackles of my journey began as I was forced to witness his barrage of blows on my mother. These acts of violence and aggression left an indelible impression upon my mind that not even an ocean of ink could dispel, for the rest of my life. I was held captive by the fear of losing my mother, suspended in shock, as I watched him beat her lifelessly and watched her rolled up into a helpless lump as   blood gushed from her head and face. Thoughts raced through my antagonized mind, and I screamed for help silently as the tears rolled down my cheeks. The verbal and physical abuse continued and I shivered with fright as I feared for my own life. I promised myself at that tender age, that I would defend and protect her with my own life. Today, the thought of her being abused, evoke the surge of anger within, especially if I see a woman being overpowered and abused by a man.

My father left the home, and we were left to survive on our own. Life was tough and we were drowning in frustration and poverty, but I was relieved that the beatings were now over. As we struggled, resentment started to set in, my mother's, spirit was tattered and bruised but she continued to look for ways and means to survive. She held on tenaciously to her God, as she looked for help from above. I guess that was the only source that she could trust since the hope she had in my father was completely gone. She had to pick up the pieces of her life and try to support herself and me.   At the age of five, I was expected to begin kindergarten. We had moved to Bellevue, but there were no schools with kindergarten facilities, I felt like a caged bird, flapping its wings to be free.

Bellevue was stigmatized by the location of the community's mental health facility, labeling it as the mad house of the country. And there I was a resident of Bellevue, to be branded for the rest of my life. I fear the very thought of someone asking me about my childhood for fear that they will run in the opposite direction. It is not the brand of clothing that any one wants to wear, neither is it the thought of being there, that anyone wants to cherish. It is a place that must not be mentioned or you could be looked upon with disdain for life.

I have traveled frequently and extensively as an adult, but Bellevue has preceded me far and wide. On one of my trips out of town I was questioned about my documents, which bear the district of Bellevue.

"Are you from Bellevue?"

"Yes," I replied, and the eyes of my interrogator never left me. Realizing what was happening, I relished the humor and said, "I was born there and have lived there for 29 years. But they gave me enough medicine and discharged me so that I can mingle with the outside world."

The stamp went all over my documents while the eyes remained on me, and they tried hurriedly to get me out of the way.

My mother taught me many stories about Jesus and his love and took me to church every Sabbath. And at the age of seven, I gave my heart to Jesus and wanted to be baptized. But like most parents, my mother felt that I was too young. I tried to convince her that I understood the message and the purpose that God had for my life, but she firmly refuted my desire and intentions.

This did not discourage me, though it delayed my excitement and joy for a while. The next time there was a baptism, I expressed my desire to be baptized, I was determined that this time I was going to get my way. On the day of the baptism, I ran ahead of the crowd into the river and waited for the officiating minister and his associates to enter the water. In those days, churches did not have the luxury of having a baptismal pool in the church; they either used a river to conduct their baptismal service or did it by the sea. I accosted the minister, holding him around the legs with great determination, despite the rebuke and refute of the elders of the church. My mother knew that I was determined to be baptized and, despite the sentiments of those around, she consented for the minister to baptize me.

I was so happy as I went down into the water and when I came up I was singing in my little heart, "Sweet Jesus, Sweet Jesus what a wonder you are," and I held that name with such delight for as long as I can remember.

The common thread that now glued my mother and me together was the inner peace that was given from above. My mother continued to teach me about the goodness of God but I needed to go to school where I could have a formal education. We moved to the district of Windsor   seven   miles   away,   from   Bellevue.
I was very excited about school and was well-loved by

my teachers and the staff, who often remarked about my obedience and willingness as a child.

I was always ready to do whatever task that was assigned to me by my teacher and felt that I was special and well favored. I was very short in stature and was left out of the most popular game that was played by boys in the West Indies- "cricket" The game of cricket was played during recess and lunchtime. I stuck around the classroom and was willing to run any errands for the teacher. One day, the bigger boys were so engaged in their game of cricket, that they were rather late in coming back to class. The teacher told me to go out and call them in and told me that if they refused to come in, I had permission to pull up the wickets. I felt great. I was on top of the world I was actually given some authority and I was ready to use it. I stepped outside with a great sense of pride, and told them that they needed to be inside for class. They ignored me! I could not believe it! They actually pretended I was not even there and continued to play. So I marched right over and yanked up the wickets as I was told to do. I stood tall as my face flickered with delight. It felt great being in charge. Suddenly the smile was whisked from my cheek and stars of every color captured my vision as I felt a massive blow to my head. One of the bigger boys had wacked me from behind with a bat. And then I was out cold. I fell unconscious, bleeding from my head, and I had to be rushed to the nearest hospital.

The facilities at the hospital in Port Antonio were not adequate to treat such emergency so I had to be sent to another hospital in Kingston, (the capital of Jamaica) where I laid unconscious for three days. However, somewhere in this unconscious state, I heard my mother's voice as she prayed for me. I could distinctly remember hearing my mother telling God that if He would spare my life, that she would give me back to Him for service. Almost immediately, I opened my eyes and saw the nurse moving around the room.

I was in great pain. I tried to look around, trying to understand while, questioning the experience that brought me there. My head throbbed severely. My heart beat thunderously, as I shook violently at the thought of what had happened to me. I was in and out of a consciousness. The nurse told my mother that my eyes were opened. She asked me if I was hungry, and I told her I was, so she brought me something, but I couldn't have very much. After a few days in the hospital, I was told that I could now   do the basics in attending to my personal needs. I felt good that I would now be able to take my baths without the assistance of the nurse. I tried to enter the shower room, but noticed that my vision was blurred. Eventually I could not see. Fear gripped me, as I cried out for help and I finally lapsed into a state of unconsciousness. I lost tract of time, I eventually found myself back in bed, cleaned and dressed. I heard my mother's voice and waited eagerly for her, for she was the comfort that I needed, the only world that I knew.

After a few more days, I was transferred back to the Port Antonio hospital to recuperate but this was to be the most disturbing part of my shackled journey to recovery. The medical diagnosis was that the brain was damaged and it seemed like I was slated to be a damaged cargo for the rest of my life. Because of the extent of my head injury, the doctor told my mother that it was useless sending me back to school, because I would not be able to learn anything and would be mentally impaired and challenged for the rest of my life.

Out of fear and concern, my mother kept me at home until I was 17 years old. At this point, I felt that I was able to learn and I decided to return to school, which would have given me only one year to complete school since age 18 was the last year to complete school based on the educational system. I took advantage of this last year through advanced studies without any major problems.

Years later I started to experience difficulty. I had a number of seizures, but after much prayer the medical evaluation showed no evidence of internal damage to my brain. I can only credit this miracle to God, Who is still in the miracle business today.

I promised myself that because God had spared my life and granted my mother her request, that I would not disappoint Him but would gladly surrender to His will.

I failed to keep my promise. I was distracted and discouraged while attending church. I wanted to feel as though I belonged. I wanted to feel loved, but my confidence and hope were destroyed. I was tired of what life had to offer me. I was branded as a cast out, a nuisance and menace to society. My father had cursed the church and now I was seen as the apple of his eye, the chip that fell from his shoulder. I was hurting deeply I just needed someone to show me love, compassion and understanding. I wanted to move away from the life my father had shown me. I needed to find hope and felt like the church had let me down.

The biggest mistake I made was to put my trust and confidence in man. I didn't know that I was to hope in the God of the universe. It was at a communion service that I publicly turned my back on God. I was falsely accused of disturbing the communion service and I threw away the communion bread and walked right out of the presence of God. I did not realize that I had just tightened the shackles that held me like a caged bird. I felt like life was nothing but a merry- go- round. I did not know which way to turn. I was held by the stake of uncontrollable cords of fear, rejection and poverty. I left my mother's home and went to look for a livelihood. I desperately wanted to take care of her, but the threads that held the cords of, rejection, and despair continued to lock their grip around me as I ventured out into the open arms of failure that waited to engulf me like a seething lion. I soon found myself on a political bandwagon. Before long, I was one of the boys in the nation's ruling party. I felt like I was riding in high places and it felt great. The doors of opportunity were now open, well that was what I thought, but that did not last for very long, for my party lost the general election, and I went back on poverty lane.   Although my party lost the elections, I held great admiration and respect for the elected prime minister. I was so impressed with him as a leader that at one of his rally I ran up on the stage to greet him. He asked me what I wanted to do for him and I told him I wanted to sing a song. This was a popular song that was done at all his campaigns. He gave me so much commendation and even had the crowd cheering for me. I was on top of the world. Never in my whole life had I felt so good about myself. My self esteem was elevated and I cherished that moment for a very long time. After all that celebration was over I was back at the drawing board. There was nothing out there for me and nothing to appeal to me.

I was literally choking from life's horrifying experience. I was stifled by the vicious and cruel attack of the experiences in life. I returned to visit my mother. Upon approaching, I heard uproar with two of my childhood friends and one of the elders of the church. Unfortunately they had a problem discussing the fact that there was glaring evidence that he killed their dog because traces of blood led directly to his home. A fight broke out and one of the guys hit him with a piece of stick and broke his leg. They quickly left the district but I didn't leave since I was not the one who did it. A few days later I was walking down the street and was suddenly surrounded by four police cars. Apparently he had a relative who was a police officer who visited him while he was in the hospital. He told him that since the other guys had left then I would have to suffer the consequences. He told him that I had attacked him with an M16 rifle and held the gun on him while the other boys beat him and broke his leg. My miseries were about to multiply.

The sounds of sirens filled the air. I was hand-cuffed and arrested. They held me at the station for seven days. I tried to explain that I was falsely accused but they just ignored me. I told myself not to worry, since my uncle was a police officer and would be on duty that very afternoon. As soon as my uncle stepped in I braced myself for relief, for he was my mother's brother and would surely take care of me. I was shocked when he came in and did not even acknowledge me, apparently he must have been embarrassed. He later asked me what happened but never said a word to my mother. It was another police officer who informed her of my arrest and had an attorney arranged for them to post bail.

At the hearing, the accuser told the judge that I was carrying a M-16 in my waist and a piece of stick and some stones in my hand. The ridiculous story merely amused the judge when he asked for the scene to be replayed by having someone re-enact it. The case was thrown out, and the accuser was chased out of the court-house. The judge told me that I could sue this man, but my mother who was in court with me spoke up and said there was no need to do that, because God would take care of the situation. It is always good to let God fight your battles because he never loses. Six months later the same man got a stroke and was paralyzed. A few months later his wife became ill and died. God was fighting for me because I was helpless. He was taking care of me but I was too busy to notice.

I thought about the fact that my mother was a Godly woman with a very with humble beginning. I thought about the horrifying experiences she endured during childhood. She had been a very sick child; this prevented her from going to school to obtain an education. Now I had to dispel the shackles of poverty, as our lives seemed destined to be.

My thoughts roamed back to the story she told me that at the age of 16 she was stricken with a serious illness that paralyzed her hands and feet for four and a half years, forcing her to crawl like a creature to move from one place to another. In order to eat, she had to lap up her food like a dog until she was 18. Despite the fact that she had the ability to produce the most beautiful hand-crafted work, she still could not provide a steady income to support our daily needs.

I knew I had to make a turning point in my life when I witnessed my mother going from door to door in the neighborhood, seeking assistance from the neighbors to provide for our well-being, and one of the neighbors slammed the door in her face. I considered that act a gross insult to human decency, and my heart felt as if it was breaking into pieces. I told God that He had to do something to help us. I vowed that day that I would try to cushion my mother from such embarrassment, and I was determined in my mind that there were two things I would never do when I became a man. I vowed that I would never inflict pain or abuse a woman, as my own father did. And I would never leave or ill-treat my mother in any way, hoping that I could make up for some of the hardness and pain she had to suffer just for me.

Chapter II

Break through and Show me the way

I had to find a way out. I was really getting tired of the sickening pattern with our life. Something had to be done or I would have to make some radical changes in my life. I pondered over the situation and reflected on when I was 12; instead of being in school I was searching for odd jobs to support my mother and myself. I was tired of it and needed a change. For years my family stood in the way of me obtaining a job to provide food. There was no support from anywhere although I was only two feet in stature. I went to look for work at the Forest Bank and took my cutlass along with me. My friends joked around that my cutlass was the same size as I was.

I thought about how God came through for me, and I got the job, carrying water and cutting grass. It was not much but I was happy I had an honest job, and that nobody would have to slam doors in my mother's face ever again. We were paid every fortnight, and when I received my pay envelope, I went straight home and gave it to my mother, but held something so that I could buy my first bottle of soda for then I felt a sense of manhood, as the provider of the home. But after working for some time, I made new friends and wanted to hang out with the boys at the pub on paydays. I began holding back 20 dollars of my wages as pocket money so I could hang out with the boys.

I soon remembered who I was: a poor boy, the son of violent drunkard with two strikes against me. Two strikes that were deeply buried in my genes, just waiting to hold me shackled, to my inherited poverty-stricken life. I was determined to become nobody's fool, wasting my earnings in riotous living. I figured out a plan where I did not allow any of my friends to buy me a drink. If they bought me a drink, I would have to reciprocate by buying each one of them a beer from my already meager means. I would drink with them, making sure to let them see me buy one beer and as we talked and laughed. I would excuse myself whenever the beer bottle was almost empty and fill it with water each time, before returning to the table. I was able to drink with them, pretending even to get drunk from the repeated drinking, just to be a part of the crowd. But my resolution was sealed that I would not leave my mother alone.

Although she had two brothers, the one who was a district constable did not have time to think about us. He had even tried to prevent me from getting the job at the Forest Bank and discouraged my mother from taking care of me. I thought about all of this and remembered how   God came through for us, as my other uncle who lived in England would send some assistance periodically. God had seen us through some rough times, but here I was just coming out of jail trying to ask him to show me the way.   I was reminded of the psalmist's thoughts, "I have never seen the righteous forsaken, nor his seed begging bread" (Ps 37:25).

But my heart was now hardened against the church and I could no longer hear   the voice of God or see the purpose for my life. I started to hang out with my friends even more and   found myself on a path that was heading for destruction. It was close to election time for new leadership in the country. I was very excited about election and   I decided to make connections with my political friends. I found my self with a new zeal. I attended the political forums and campaigned with zeal for I had found where I truly **belong** so I thought. I got close with one Member of Parliament of the ruling party. The compass of life started to change and I felt that I was on the right tract. Life was good and I relished the life of plenty. This did not last very long. My friend's Party had now lost the elections and he was now financially crippled. He told me about a deal. He had to market pounds of marijuana and that inspired me to work my own deal. I was now trapped in a dangerous ring. I got some of my friends who grew the plant to credit me 1400 pounds with a street values of approximately 1.5 million dollars. I worked in both disposing the drug and securing the cash. This was heavy drug trafficking. We hired three police officers to work with us to avoid any suspicion. One of my friend's nephews arranged for a small aircraft to transport the drugs to another country. The drug was securely stored until they could load it to the aircraft. God was about to show me that that was not his way for me and so the plan was interrupted by His divine hand. The sound of gunshots rang throughout the area. There was a gun battle between some policemen and some gun men. This mandated a search and sure enough the ganja was found before it got to the aircraft. It was confiscated and leaving us with a loss of 1.5 million dollars to repay. I felt like I was going to lose my mind. Where would I get that kind of money to repay and to whom would I go?

One of the guys working with us owned a block factory so he arranged to repay the 1.5 million a little at a time. Sure enough he went bankrupt and had to leave the country. I was now left to assume the responsibility in repaying the rest of the bill. The other guys were quite supportive but that did not change the fact that I was broke and destitute. I tried to find some of my other political friends and discovered that the ruling political party had organized a special guerilla force as body-guard and since we were the rivals of that governing party we became their main target... One night they broke in to the home of one of my friends, dragged him out of his bed, and carried him out away into the bushes where they beat him mercilessly. Luckily he was able to drag himself to the main road and eventually hiked a ride back home. We were in constant fear for our lives and we took to the mountains and remained there until things cooled down a little.

We decided to leave one morning to go to another town. We agreed to meet at a certain place and time but I overslept and the group left without me. Little did I know that God's hand was in it. They left me a note that I could join them on the next trip. About two days later a news broadcast announced that five men were gunned down and killed. I became fearful because I realized that the identified bodies were those of my friends. I was now left from the group. I still tried to find the way. I needed to chart a path that could lead me to the life that I so long desire. I turned in a different direction, with no hope no money and no home.

I went in search of some other friends. I had to ride the bus so I told the driver that my father had died and I needed to get to the town of Port Morant. I knew my friends would be there but I found them smoking marijuana. I was in such bad shape that I joined them for awhile. Shortly after that I got a job harvesting coconuts and went on to experimenting with planting seeds at a nursery. I soon became an integral part of their group with all their fun activities and finally became involved with a woman not knowing that she was the girlfriend of one of the policemen who had previously arrested me. His jealous rage led to a confrontation and I was thrown in jail for assaulting a police officer. Evidently the path that I had chosen was leading me in the way of destruction. The Police officer who had helped me the first time was now promoted to a higher rank and was again my savior. He dropped the charges and told me to get out of town.

I took his advice and decided to go into the city. I knew only one guy there in the city of Kingston and I searched and found him with some friends. He told me that they had no money and could not help me but they were planning a bank robbery and I was welcome to join in. They had 9 millimeter guns and 22 caliber pistols. One 22 caliber was placed in my hands. My mother's prayers haunted me. I prayed and asked God to show me a way of escape. My Christian commitment taunted me. Bundles of scripture tumbled in my head bringing back to reality and the path that God wanted to lead me in. I asked God to help me as I planned my escape. I listened intently to all the plans for the robbery and gave all indications that I was in on the deal. As soon as they were gone to sleep, I made my escape through the window with only the clothing on my back.

I waded through muddy water under a bridge. I knew I had a mission, for I felt that God was showing me the way of escape. I hid in the dark in the cold damp water and took shelter there until daybreak. My mind flickered back on a Pastor that I know some time ago and so I decided to start the long search. After hours of inquiry, I was given direction to his house. When I got there, I was told that he would not be home until after service because he was holding a series of meeting. I was hungry and tired but I decided to walk the eight miles to the pastor's office and planned that I would present my critical situation to him at the end of the service. I was weak from hunger, tired from the exhausted journey desperate for a change to find the way to the right path. At the end of his message, the pastor made an appeal. I made my way to the altar with the hope that I would get an opportunity to speak with him.

After the service, I poured out my heart and made my petition. He told me that he could not help but I decided that under no circumstance was he going to leave me there. I ran ahead of him and sat in the back seat of his car, and refused to get out despite his insistence. He realized that I was desperate and he spoke to his wife and she consented for me to stay with them for a limited time of three days. I was so ecstatic; my heart was filled with gratitude. I arose early that morning from 4oclock and started to clean their kitchen that was already clean. After that, I washed their car and tried to make myself useful just to show my gratitude and appreciation for what they were doing for me.

As we sat at the breakfast table, the conversation was interrupted by the breaking news forecast of a bank robbery. I drifted into a daze and faintly heard the shocking news that five men were shot dead in a bank robbery and I knew they were my friends. I started to cry because these were the very friends I had ran away from. The horrifying news suspended my appetite. Thoughts of God's merciful hand flooded my mind. I was convinced that God had brought me this far to show me the path that He wanted me to take. I purposed in my heart that I would be in the next baptism. I asked the pastor for the date and he told me it would be in three weeks and I made a another vow to God because he had proven himself to be my deliverer, and had brought me to this point in my life and there was no turning back. That morning the pastor took me to a restaurant owned and managed by a sister and her husband from the church. He tried to seek employment for me and since they had just released their gardener, that job was now available to me. I was delighted that I now had job with room and board. Unfortunately, I had to eat my food in the backyard with the dogs. I wanted to show my gratitude for their hospitality so I decided to extend my responsibility and assisted them with the work in the restaurant.

The pastor always came by to take me to church. I had bought a suit of clothing for church, which I wore every Sabbath. I now had one set of clothing for church and one for work. I felt that my journey for success had now begun. Although I did not approve of the dehumanized treatment, I believe that God was trying to tell me something. I was humbled by the environment in which I had to eat but nonetheless grateful, for the opportunity to gradually rise above a certain level of dependency. An opportunity had presented itself for me to move a step above my designated position. I figured that if I worked well in the kitchen I would soon impress upon my boss that I was worthy of notice and promotion. I relished the thought of breaking through my lowly state and shared my dreams with my boss's son. We had grown close to each other as brother since we were both the same age. I knew he understood my pains and shared my eagerness to move up the ladder of success. Positive dreams saturated my thoughts and I thank God for leading me into the path of success.

Chapter III

His hand on my life

Somehow I felt that the Lord had His hand on my life. I was now ready to do his will. My employer's son was like the brother I never had, and I was happy that life had regained its rightful position in my experience. One day my employers were expecting some out-of-town guests, and their son was asked to pick them up from the airport. He asked me if I wanted to go with him, and I gladly agreed to accompany him to the airport. When we returned his mom railed with anger, in front of her guests, at the thought of me going with her son, to pick them up. Every ounce of happiness drained out of my body. Was this really happening to me? Was I not good enough to meet and greet their guests? Their son was just as stupefied as I was. A million thoughts came rushing in my mind and I wondered whether it was God's hand on my life or His wrath to reposition me for what was to come.

One of the guests questioned whether or not something was wrong with me why my boss was so annoyed about me going to the airport. The feeling of inferiority complex swept through my being. I turned and asked my employer, before leaving them, if something was wrong with me, or whether I was inferior to them. Instantly, all the old thoughts came rushing back into my mind, as I asked myself how could such people who held such high positions in the church, as first elder and church ministries leader, treat me this way? I did not realize that my ultimate example should be Christ Himself. I did not know that my trust should only be in God. I should have known from my past experience that the church will host both the good and the bad and that discouragement will come to test our faith. I was not concerned about the reality of life. I was consumed with the passion of living a comfortable and happy life. I felt that every drop of peace and contentment had leaked through the cracks. I went to bed that night and questioned the path that God had mapped out for me. I questioned his hand on my life. I asked him for more grace and strength to carry on.

The following morning, my boss told me that I had to cook breakfast and set the table for 13, and I was happy to do the job. I felt that the previous day's experience was already swept under the carpet and we were now ready to move forward. I set the table not just for 13 but 14 for I figured she had forgotten that I needed to set a place for myself. The way I figured it, God made us all equal and there is no way she would let her guest know that I was not welcomed to eat at the family table. After all, I was good enough to fix the meal there is no reason why I could not eat with them.   After everybody had occupied their seats, it left one vacant because I had gone downstairs to take my bath and change into more appropriate attire. When I returned, my employer told me she needed to have a word with me. I was quite baffled because I knew I had done what she had asked.

I was furious when I realize what her intentions were so for the first time, I refused to do what she said and remained at the table. I thought that the fact that I had an audience she would be courteous and not do what she intended to do. I told her that whatever she had to say to me could be said right in the presence of all who were there, and I was not prepared to eat with the dogs in the backyard anymore, because I didn't look like them. I reminded her that I had two hands and two feet just like the people around that table, and I was no different from them. But she insisted that I could not eat at the table. I told her that if I couldn't eat at the table, then nobody was going to eat because I would turn the table over. I knew that was not the right thing to do. In fact God asked us to represent him even when we are tempted to do the wrong. My past experience flooded my thoughts for a while and my eyes burned with anger. It was then that one of the guests intervened and said that we could work this out. But I told her that I was quitting and that I was going downstairs to collect my things and that she should have my two weeks pay ready in an envelope with my name on it. This experience was quite belittling and embarrassing for me.

Upon my return I received my two weeks pay and I left, again with no place to go. Tears rolled down my cheek as I asked "where is God in all of this? My god was always there. He promised that He would always be there I was just not aware of His presence. Sometimes when we are going through our valley experience we forget that He is there. He is right there with us cheering us to go on. The experiences of life are just the stepping stones for a smoother path, but who wants to walk on a rocky road? I went back to the pastor, and I explained the situation. He said that he could not take me in, but that there was an old building, without windows or doors, to which I was welcomed. I accepted it and made myself as comfortable as I could, with the gift of an old single bed from a lady who pitied my homeless plight.

I continued to go to church every Sabbath in my one suit and sat at the very back of the church to make it easier for me to leave when the service ended before anybody had an opportunity to treat me contemptuously. I had no friends at church, I felt alone and nobody even tried to speak to me until one Sabbath, a young man who seemed   as lonely and friendless as I was, came and spoke to me. I told him my situation and after talking with him for a while he asked if I wanted to stay with him and his grandmother.

My new friend, was employed at a bank and received a special banking allowance, which he shared with me and helped me to buy some new clothes. We became very good friends and lived like brothers for about five years. He did everything that he could for me, even sending me back to school where I pursued a course in quality control and food processing.

The course required the prerequisites of three General Certificate of Education, or GCE, O-levels, which I did not have. But I was determined to put God to the test, to prove that nothing is impossible with Him. I told the authorities at the school that I had a B.A. degree and an H.S. degree. I expected them to question my qualification. Why would I be there with a bachelor's degree? I most likely would be more qualified than the one's who worked there at the time. There were 42 prospective students, but only 8 of us passed the test. I was thrilled, because I knew that it was the leading of the Lord. I beamed with excitement but I knew that very soon, I would be asked to presents my diploma and certificates. I was scared because I had nothing to show. I prayed and asked God to tell me what to say. The night before the interview I pleaded with my God because I needed him to show me the way and tell me what to do in order to remain there.

Close to the end of the course I was summoned to the office and asked to bring my qualifications along. I went and took my seat before the manager and looked her directly in the face with a smile. She acknowledged me and asked for my credentials. I told her that I did not bring them. I said that my father held my documents, and he would not give them to me. So she told me to have my father bring them into the office. I told her that my father was there, and since she did not see anyone on the inside, she told me to go out and have him come in with the documents. I told her that he was right there inside, and that she could ask him for them.

"Where is he?" she inquired.

"Right here, standing right beside me and His name is Jesus," I said.

She drew back from the desk, looked at me, quite befuddled and said she needed to call the director at once. I started to tremble because even though I believed that God would work things out, I feared at the thought of being humiliated in front of others.

In a few minutes both ladies returned, and this time it was the director who spoke to me. She said, "Mr. Somers, how are you?"

"I'm fine, Madam," I replied.

"You said you hold two degrees, and we must see your original certificate in order to process your papers for the course."

"Yes, madam. I have a B.A degree, because I am Born Again, and an H.S. degree, by the Holy Spirit. Jesus is my ultimate Father who holds these documents for me. He never gives them to me to keep."

The director bowed her head and smiled warmly before saying, "Very well, you have been here for almost six weeks, and you have completed the course. I guess we could move on from here." She also told me that my performance was outstanding, and that I had done exceptionally well in the course, and as a result, they would allowed me to use the school's facilities to begin processing my goods.

I began my own company which I called, "Harvest Time," where I preserved diced papaya, made papaya syrup, sorrel syrup, and papaya jam. I wanted to expand my business, so I approached some of the brethren from the church with samples of my products, soliciting prospective sponsors for my business. Three of them were willing to join me as partners.

I realized that in order for the business to grow, I needed a wider market for my goods. Therefore I went on a two week marketing campaign outside of the country. But upon my return, I discovered that some of the very men who worked for me had sold the processing formula to another company and closed down my business. I was devastated. Here was a chance for me to excel on my own and now my dream was all crumbled. I called a meeting with them on two occasions, but they did not show up. I contacted the pastor of the church, hoping that he would be able to bring us together to discuss the matter, but again, nobody showed up. The pastor told me that it was totally out of his control and that I should take the matter up with the court to seek some form of compensation. I decided against his advice because we were all brethren of the faith, and I did not want to bring the church into disrepute because a few men chose to dishonor the righteousness of the faith.

Chapter IV

Here am I send me

I was back to square one. No money, no job no means of survival. I went back to my friend who at that time was treasurer of the church. He advised me to look into getting involved with some evangelistic work in the community and we began with house to house visitation. I felt that I was finally doing what I was called to do.

One day we knocked on a door, and a very beautiful young lady responded. We soon learned that she had lived a very destitute life, and was seeking for positive changes in her life. She requested bible studies after we spoke with her, and soon she was baptized and became a good friend to both of us. However, whenever she visited us at home, she would always be dressed in a very revealing and seductive manner. I noticed that she was bonding very closely with my friend and soon realized that it was more than a casual friendship between them.

One day as she sat opposite to us, she began to make enticing gestures, ensuring that she held our attention as she moved her hands along the border of her mini skirt, as if luring us to be her prey. This was a very tempting and befuddling experience for both of us, for neither my friend or I had yet experienced personal relationships with the opposite sex. She beckoned to my friend who soon became a captive to her trap. I immediately became the outsider in the very place I called home. My friend and I grew apart since he had to spend more time with his new found love.

I watched from a distance as my friend became more and more entangled in the relationship with her and we drifted apart from even the spiritual experience that we once shared. I eventually realize that I was no longer welcomed in his home. He finally told me to find somewhere else to live. He explained that he needed some privacy and I told him that I totally understood. What I did not understand, was the way in which God was working. Every time I felt like I was making progress, something would always go wrong. I could not understand that maybe God was doing all of this to prepare me for service. Again I became homeless and penniless. But not long thereafter, my friend came to me seeking my help, because he did not want to lose his position in the church.

After what seemed to be a long discussion with him, he confessed to me that the same lady was pregnant for him. He wanted me to accompany her to a clinic out of town to get an abortion. I was baffled at the fact that he had gotten her pregnant but even more stupefied at the thought of an abortion. This was murder and to be committed by Christians, this was more than I could bear. Not a very pleasant task to ask of a friend, but how could I refuse, when he had done so much for me? So I took her to the doctor.

I felt like I had to do this favor to help my friend, but deep down I felt guilty because I knew it was wrong. I looked at the way I was living. I decided to change my way of living   but in a few months my friend was back to ask me to take this woman to abort another baby. "Enough is enough" I said to my self and I told him that I made the mistake the first time but will not do it the second time. I told him that if he really loved the lady, then he needed to marry her, but I was not going to help him again to destroy a life.

I continued to go to church but then as I sat there one day, I was suddenly hit with the reality of rejection. I realized that everybody else had been asked to participate in the work of the church except me, beads of anger poured out of my thoughts. Nobody saw the worth in me, not even my friend who was the treasurer of the church. Evidently he could not persuade any one to look at my potentials. He could not even persuade the other leaders to include me in their company. I was left there as a lonely and rejected misfit.

One night, I had a dream that my friend and I were walking through a beautiful open field, with green grass and exotic plants and flowers surrounding the circumference of the land. I realized that the voice I was hearing as we walked and talked was not that of friend any longer, for my friend had turned out to be a strange man walking beside me clad in pure white from the waist down, which was all I could see.

But He said to me, "Look up and tell me what you see."

And I looked up and replied, "I see a stone."

He said, "Can you see anything else? Look up again and tell me what you see."

I said, "I see a stone, a large stone."

"Can you see what is holding the stone?" he asked.

I said, "It looks like a piece of thread, yes it is a piece of thread."

And he said, "Can you see the stone hanging over the feet of a man? When the stone falls upon the feet of the man, it means that this world will come to an end."

But I was feeling very afraid and so I said, "Call my friend and show it to him."

He said, "Don't worry about your friend."

As I looked across the field, I saw my friend standing on the other side, with a river between us. Then the man's voice said to me, "Go home and study the books of Daniel and Revelation, and then you will understand all the things that I have said to you."

When I woke up I was very frightened, but I had a longing desire to study the two books, Daniel and Revelation. I read them over and over again until I could almost recite them verbatim. But for some reason I was troubled, because I did not know how to accomplish the task that was given to me. I tried to do all that I could in the church, I told the leaders about my dream but they never gave me an opportunity to tell my dream or encouraged me regarding its meaning, and I could not understand why. I was totally despised and rejected, and I felt like my childhood experience were about to be relived.

I felt shackled by my circumstances and could not do anything about it. I tried to seek God's face but His timing is not always ours. I wanted things to be nice and rosy but was sadly reminded of the path Christ had to take. He was rejected of men and he walked the plank of poverty. He had nothing of His own and the thought of his experience gave me a little hope. One day, however, two elderly sisters of the church called me and said that every Sunday morning they had an early prayer meeting. They asked me to join them. I was delighted, for nobody had ever asked me to do anything like that before, not knowing that God was preparing me for His mission in the future.

Soon it was time for the election of church officers for the incoming year, and I was overlooked again. No one saw the worth or potential in me.   But I remained true to my faith and to my God, finding myself seated every Sabbath in the back seat of the church.

One night I had another dream, only this time it was in the church. In the midst of the service, the same strange man, dressed in white from the waist down, entered the building. His footsteps could be heard as he firmly walked to the front of the church. He came in and he elected everybody in the church, every boy and girl, and gave them a position, except me. And as I heard his Voice, I recognized it to be the same voice that had showed up and spoken to me in the open field

when he was finished, I took up my Bible and pointed it at him, and said, "You have given everybody in this church a position, but you did not give me one. But I want you to know that Jesus has already given me my position, and not even you can take it away from me." I walked out of the church and onto the street with my open Bible, telling everybody that passed by that Jesus loves them, that Jesus is coming again, and that they must get ready to go with Jesus when He comes.

But the dream continued, I dreamt that on the following Sabbath, during the vesper service, the same strange man, dressed in white with an apron over his shirt, walked up to the pulpit and asked the church elder, "Who is the pastor in this church?"

The elder replied, "I think that's me."

"You think that's you?"

"Yes."

"Well, do you have a young man in this congregation by the name of Joseph Somers?"

The elder said, "I think so."

"You think so?"

"Yes, I think so."

And then the strange man turned and said, "Is there anybody here by the name of Joseph Somers?"

I was sitting at the back of the church. I said, "Yes sir," and I stood up.

He said, "Could you join me up here?"

I could not see a face, only his body from the waist down, but I joined him.

He said to the congregation, "Can everybody see this young man?"

They replied, "Yes."

He said, "In case anybody misses him, please turn the lights up higher." They turned the lights up higher, like a floodlight, which made the inside of the church look like bright daylight. He continued speaking. "And now, since everybody can see him, let me do what I was sent to do." He put his hand into the pocket of his apron and took out a vial. But the vial was so bright and shining like sparkled gold that nobody could bear to look upon it. Then he uncapped the vial and poured the oil that was inside of it over my head. It was so much oil that it made a puddle all around me. And as he poured the oil over my head he said, "Now I have anointed you as a missionary from this day forward until the day that you die," and then he disappeared as strangely as he came.

In my dream, I was so afraid that I started to tremble and wondered what would happen to me. Who was that man, and why me? Did he hate me? Why didn't he call me up when he was there the first time, when he selected everybody else? Why only me, what was I suppose to do now?

When I awoke the next morning I realized that it was only a dream. I began to settle down, thinking it would soon go away. But I distinctly remembered what the man had said, although I did not know what he meant. The following week, I went to the conference office looking for something, anything that I could find to do that would give me a little money. I met a pastor that I had known from my boyhood.

He said to me, "Somers come and do a crusade for me."

I said, "Sure."

He said, "Put your topics together for the nightly service. Next Sabbath, I want to present you to the church, so come prepared to preach."

I said, "Sure."

Now, I had never preached before, not even to speak in a church. And I certainly did not know anything about any topics or how to put them together. So I went out and sat under a big tree in the conference office's yard, and I said, "Now Lord, I do not know how to preach. I never preached before, never had the chance to learn, but I accepted this by faith."

Then I saw a good friend of mine, a young pastor, coming into the yard. I called out to him. "Pastor, I need to talk to you, man," and I told him about my dilemma.

He smiled as always and said, "I will show you how to put your topics together and line them up," and he did.

But I was still nervous, because now I had to prepare for a preaching assignment on the Sabbath, and I didn't know where to begin – or end, for that matter. Then a day later, a friend told me about a preacher who was holding a crusade in Saint Andrew, and I decided to attend the nightly meetings. I copied all of his sermons and matched them up with the line-up from my pastor friend.

Sabbath came. I was presented at the church and was introduced as the speaker for the divine hour. So I said in my heart, *"Lord"?* I know I stood up, and I know a few minutes later I sat down, but I don't know to this day what I said. The members all came up to me and praised me, saying surely I was anointed. But this was soon to be proven, as the crusade began and these same people who said I did such a fine job did not come out to the nightly meetings. And I knew why. I knew deep down that they did not think that I was qualified enough to preach to them.

The crusade was ten miles from where I was boarding, and I had no means of transportation from the place where the church pastor put me to stay for the duration of the meetings. The church pastor also did not provide my host with money for my room and board. I said to myself, *Lord, is this what being a missionary is all about?*

The sister with whom I was boarding gave me my meals. But her husband, who was the sole provider, fell ill and laid sick for about three weeks, so his wife had to find a way to provide for the family. They had three cows, and neither the wife nor I knew how to feed these cows, but I was the only male hand around the house, so I had to help with the feeding of the cows and any other chores to help out my host. Not knowing how to cut the grass or pack them, I bundled them in my shirt and carried them on my head, not knowing that they would itch. Yes, shackled and itching.

On the opening night of the crusade, I walked the ten miles to the church and then walked ten miles back, And I said, "Lord, this isn't missionary work, this is punishment," and to make matters worse, only five people and some little children showed up every night. Nobody wanted to hear me; they did not think I was qualified for the job.

But although I was discouraged, there was one man who helped me to continue preaching. He was there every night, though he had only one foot. Then on the last night of the first week, he came to me and said he knew why the people were not coming out and why he was faithfully supporting me. And he shared his testimony. Some time ago, his friends invited him to attend meetings just like the one I was conducting, and he would constantly hide from them every time they came by to pick him up. One evening when his friend came for him, he went up in an ackee tree to pick ackees. While trying to pick the ackees that were hanging far out on the limb, he lost his balance and fell, His leg got caught in the crutch of the tree ,and unfortunately his leg was broken. The damage to his leg was so extensive that the leg had to be amputated. But the very night that he was discharged from the hospital, the crusade was still going on. He made his way to the meetings on one foot and had been ever faithful from that day, never missing a night. He was always there to assemble the chairs and do anything else that needed to be done, although he had only one foot.

I used this man's testimony, and every night since then the church members began coming out to support the meetings. But my friend with the one foot told me that the pastors of the First Day Churches told their members not to come to the meetings. I decided to go and see the pastors and try to befriend them. I started attending their churches. The Church of God pastor saw me in the congregation and invited me to preach for them. They sent the moderator down in the congregation to escort me to the pulpit and told me that the rest of the evening was mine, that there was no time limit.

I said to myself, "How do I transform *a five-minute copied sermon to a no time limit, what is this?*"

Well! I began to preach, and as I fired up real quick all the people started running to the altar, crying and speaking in unknown 'tongues', so that even I had to join them. But I soon realized that I didn't know what I was saying, so I said in a commanding voice, "CUT!"

Everybody shut up and went back to their seats. So I started to preach again, and again, things heated up real quick, and everybody was out of their seats dancing around. Soon church was out, the earliest they came out on a Sunday morning. But that Sunday evening, my crusade was filled with members from the Church of God.

Then the pastors of the church formed a band against me, calling me a sheep-stealer, saying that I tricked them, but they could not stop the people from attending the meetings. At the end of the meetings, the moderator and five others were baptized into God's Remnant Church.

When the nine weeks of the crusade was over, 12 people were baptized, but the church pastor never showed up to thank me or settle my boarding fees. I felt used and quite discouraged. I did not realize that some-times things do not go the way we want it to go. I did not realize that sometimes God put people in our path just for that time, that moment and then life goes on. I now believe that God needed me for that time and moment and then I just had to move on. I also realize that grati-tude is not a common commodity among mankind. I made my way to the place I call home. So I consoled myself that, after all, I was no preacher, and not even a good Bible worker. But I still needed to eat and live, and I could not even buy soap to wash my clothes that I had worn during the nine weeks. I had to preach every night, conduct Bible studies during the days, and assist my host with the difficult chores around the house, in apprecia-tion for her kindness.

But the Lord always provided, and one of the two elderly sisters who had invited me to the early morning prayer meetings offered to take my clothes and clean them for me. I could not help but question how God could send me on a mission and not provide for me. I said, "Lord, I don't know what I said to those people". You know I was not a preacher, but 12 of them got baptized. Surely this was worth something."

Then one day as I sat down and thought about my situation, the Holy Spirit said to me, "Go back to the evangelist whose sermons you copied, and tell him you need a job."

I could not have received better news than that, so I got up and was on my way. As I entered the office and spoke with the secretary, she said that he was busy, but that I could have a seat. I sat for a few minutes.

After hearing the receiver rest in the phone, a voice called out to the secretary, "Is someone there to see me?" The secretary was his daughter.

She replied, "Yes daddy, a young man is waiting."

As I was escorted into the room the evangelist said to me, "You look like a missionary."

I thought for a moment, *that is what the strange man said I would be.* So I said, "Yes, sir." I told him the situation and that I was looking for work.

He asked me two questions. "Are you married?"

"No, sir."

"Do you have any children?"

"No, sir."

"Then go and pack your bags and meet me back here. We are leaving for a crusade in St. Ann in a week's time, but we need to go down now to do some ground work."

Well! This was new to me. I didn't know that ground work had to be done. I was so happy, hungry, and penniless that I went home, packed my bags, and was back in no time to join the team, ready to set off on our mission. We were fed and nourished before setting off on our journey, and this was very encouraging to me to have a full stomach, for a change.

The first week was good. There was a lot of food, fun, and good fellowship, as we went about meeting the people of the community. I was convinced that God had finally paved the way. Shortly after, I got comfortable. I was on a spiritual high. I was ready to say "Here am I Lord send me." Send me in the high ways and byways, I am now fully equipped for service. Suddenly the tide began to change. The joy now started to decline, because the team was now divided and the battle became heated. There was indeed a spiritual warfare. The devil decided to rob me of my joy. I was overpowered with gloom as I was placed with an old man in an extremely humble setting.

The room was very musty and seemed not to have been occupied for many years. I gave God thanks for the humble abode and tried to make the best of it. I had no clue what my future had in store for me but I knew from the way I felt that it was going to be very challenging. My first night was quite an experience. I had a hard time finding the bathroom and decided to wait until morning to ask my host. I was literally surprised that there was no bathroom setting. I needed to go to the restroom, so I asked the brother where the toilet was.

He said. "Follow me." He led me down through a long path in the bushes to a hole that was inhabited by ferocious mosquitoes. I was immediately attacked . I wasn't sure if I was more stupefied or upset at the barbaric setting. I was frustrated and wanted to make my way of escape when I remembered that I had a mission and I swallowed my pride and allowed the tears to run freely.   This was very frustrating. I could not imagine myself using such facility. This was unheard of. I feared the attack of the army of the ferocious mosquitoes and flies. The worst part of the ordeal was the fear of me slipping down into that hole. The half was not yet told, for when the time came to wash myself, the brother offered me his basin, the only means used for a tub to take my bath. I knew this was just a temporary experience so I embraced it with joy.

That night, the devil came with a huge boulder, for while we were being transported to the crusade, the bus driver had an accident, killing himself and three other passengers. This was quite a devastating experience but amidst the attack Jehovah prevailed because we finished that crusade witnessing to 375 people who gave their hearts to the Lord in baptism.

Two months later, there was another call to go to Santa Cruz for a crusade, and I was very happy, for the folks and the team members had treated me well. So with plans ahead for the crusade, accommodations were provided that placed me this time with a wealthy family. I was quite excited for this assignment because I knew the living accommodations would be far better than the one I had before. I enjoyed the sumptuous meals everyday as my host took special care to ensure that I was well fed. One morning the host fixed breakfast, of calalou, dumplings, and bananas, and we all took our seat around the table to enjoy the meal. But as I stuck my fork in the calalou, a big worm appeared. I couldn't make an alarm, because I didn't want to embarrass my host. So I took a dumpling and covered the worm and tried to make my escape as soon as I could to feed it to the dog. I smiled to myself as I envision myself eating the worm without noticing it. I guess we don't always know what we consume especially if we did not foresee the problem. I did not bother myself about this minor problem because we had more important matters to attend to.

We were divided into twos, and I was given an elderly lady to work with. But the most exciting and trying part of our labors was with an Obeah family.

We received the cards of two young men who were attending the meetings every night, so we went in search of them and were directed to their home. On hearing who they were and where they lived, my partner refused to go, saying that it was forbidden premises. Nobody in the community would go there.

I said to her, "My sister, we must go. And I am going in Jesus' name," and she decided to join me. I was told about the woman's strange activities so I was prepared. As I arrived at the gate, I saw a coconut, a bottle of water, a cross, and a red flag. So I opened the gate, while my partner remained in the street. I went up to the door and knocked. Suddenly the door opened, and a woman appeared with a turban upon her head and pencils stuck all around it. She came out spinning her drill, three times, and I spun three times, too.

"Can I help you?" she said.

I said, "I came to see your two grandsons."

"Why do you want to see them?"

"Because they have been coming to our meetings, and they have pledged to give their hearts to Jesus. I believe that is the most honorable thing that the young men could do."

When I said that, she went to the gate and picked up the flag and the coconut and began to dance, breaking the coconut at my feet. So I began to dance too, and she began to make some sounds, so I returned the sounds to her. Then she jumped up and down and cried in the spirit, and I jumped up and down and called on the name of Jesus.

The street was now filled with spectators, because nobody had ever challenged this daughter of Beelzebub before. They were anxious to see what would happen to me. After she saw that she could not stop me, she said, "You have the spirits, too."

"No, not all of them," I said. "I know only one, and that is the Holy Ghost."

So she allowed me to see her two grandsons, who continued to come to the meetings and were baptized. Sometimes we find ourselves fearful to approach the servants of the devil, but God gives us the spirit of boldness and yet many times we are afraid to use it. He has given us the power to cast out devils, to pray for the healing of the sick and to restore the sight of the blind. The days of miracle can still be experienced if we only believe.

The power of God was again manifested one night at the meeting by a sister of the church who attended the meetings every night with her two sons. She would leave every evening before the service was over. I watched her, and one day I decided to ask her why she left before the end of the service. She told my partner and me that her husband didn't mind if her and her daughters were involved in church matters, but not his sons. So she would bring them out but try to get them home before the father got home. I told her that I would like to return and speak with the father and I asked her what was the best time to return. She said Sundays, but she advised me that it was not safe to come. I told her that I would like to give it a try. And the next Sunday, we visited the home.

As we arrived at the house and tried to open the gate, the father opened the door of the house and came out to us. "How can I help you?" he said.

I said, "We came to speak to you about your two sons."

He told us he did not want his sons involved in any church stuff, that church was for women. And he rushed back into the house and came out brandishing his cutlass.

So I told him, "I will be praying for you."

"I don't want you praying for me, I can pray for myself."

So I knelt down in the middle of the street and began to pray for him so that he could hear. I guessed he was stunned at my bravery because he disappeared by the time I was finished.

The following night the wife came to the meeting and asked, "What should I do?"

We advised her that if the boys wanted to be baptized, a private baptism could be arranged for them, and that was done. Up until that point there was no opposition from her husband. We continued to pray for him because we knew that we did not need to tell God how big the problem was but that we needed to tell the problem how big our God was.

On the last night of the crusade, I was sitting at the back of the tent, praying for souls. Suddenly the wife came to me and said, "Brother Somers, God is so good. My husband is sitting in the back of the tent on the other side." I wanted to tell her that God is a wonder working God, but I realize that she had experienced it and needed not to be reminded.

I told her to hurry and go back, that I would come around. That night I made a deal with the Lord, I said, "Lord, when the appeal is made, if you would get this man to the altar, I will get him baptized tonight."

And that night, as the appeal was made and the people were coming up, I kept my eyes focused on this man because I knew the deal that I had made with the Lord. And suddenly, I saw an angel. A woman dressed in white walked down from the altar and went straight to the man. She took him by the hand and led him to the altar like a baby. But afterwards, the woman could not be found, for the man stood at the altar alone. It was at this point I realize that I needed to say "If you can use anything Lord, You can surely use me tonight."

At the end of the appeal, one of my pastor friends and an associate prayed under the anointing with divine unction, and the man began to weep like a baby. I said to him, "Come with me, man," as I led him to the vestry. This is what the Holy Ghost told me to say to him, "Brother, tonight the Holy Spirit has led you out of spiritual Sodom, and you cannot afford to go back to Sodom because it is going to be destroyed. Don't be like Lot's wife and turn to a pillar of salt, you too can become a pillar of salt. So tonight, if you hear the voice of God, harden not your heart, and I know that you heard His voice, so please don't harden your heart."

"But I did not come prepared to be baptized." He said.

"You cannot prepare yourself to be baptized; it is the Holy Ghost that does the preparation. All you have to do is to allow Him to lead you." I said with great conviction.

"But I didn't bring a change of clothing." He continued.

I said, "Brother, you don't have a problem," so I began to take off my clothes, my shirt, and then my pants and gave them to the man, and I put on a baptismal robe.

After the man was baptized that night, people began coming from every side of the tent to be baptized. He gave his testimony, on how he tried to prevent his sons from accepting Jesus as their personal Savior. I believe that there is nothing too hard for God and that he specializes in the things that seem impossible. Sometimes we put our limit on God but He never ceases to amaze me at the things He does. Today, that brother stands as a witness He is still in the church, with his children all of whom grew up and are very active in the church.

All the glory must be to the Lord. We are only vessels to be used by him. He does not even need us because He is God all by Himself. When we are going through our Job experience and even our fiery trials, He is right there with us. Sometimes we feel that He is not even there but it is at that point that He is carrying us through the flood, the fire and our valley experiences. The three Hebrew boys (Daniel 4) exercised implicit faith when they stood up for the God whom they saw as their Deliverer. The great thing about it is that He never let us down.

Chapter V

If You Can Use Anything, Use Me

The Mountain top experience established itself far and wide because many accepted the message and the gospel mission moved to other parts of the country. At this time, it was to Water House, Kingston for another crusade in 1989.   God worked mightily as He used me to witness to the life of a little seven-year-old girl. One night after the message and the appeal was made, this little girl ran up to me saying, "Pastor, pastor, please give me one of those passport to heaven."

"Which passport, baby?" I asked.

She said, "Those in your hand," meaning the decision cards. I smiled and gave her one, and she ran out of the tent, very jubilant to give her mother the good news that she had gotten her passport to heaven. The mother scolded the child, and after she would not desist, her mother flogged her and turned on me, saying we are pressing little children, for baptism. Later that night the little girl fell very sick, vomiting uncontrollably. The ambulance was called to take her to the hospital, and as they laid her on the stretcher, she called for her older sister.

She said, "Tomorrow night, go down to the tent and ask them to give you your passport to heaven, you hear?" He uses us to reach those who should in turn reach others. That little girl knew that her time had come, and God used her to be a witness to minister to someone else.

Before the little girl reached the hospital, she died. But as a result of her sudden and unexplained death, the family members began coming to the tent and were all baptized. Each one should bring one. That is what we need to do. How often we keep His goodness to our selves. He wants us to tell somebody about the good news of salvation. There are so many souls that are thirsty for his word. Are we really willing to say "Use even me?" we need to recognize the urgency of His coming and tell someone so they can in turn tell someone else.

During that same effort, a young lady came to the meetings requesting prayer and Bible studies. But the area where she lived was depraved, and nobody frequented that part of the city because of the drugs and degeneration of the place. When the Bible counselors saw where it was, they refused to go, and they gave the request to me. I told my partner about the request, and she refused to join me right away. But after seeing my determination, she later joined me.

I knocked on the gate, and a big guy came out and said "yow what do you want? "

I told him who I was looking , and informed to him that we were there to pray for this young lady. My partner was still standing in the street, because she was afraid.

He said, "Are you a Christian?"

I said, "I am a Christian."

"Let me see how much faith you have in your God," he said as he reached in the waist of his pants from the back and pulled out a nine millimeter handgun.

"What you say if me just put this in your brain, and see if your God can take it out."

And with that my partner took off, sparing no speed. But I stood there.

"You think this is funny?"

I said, "Yes, I think it funny because the very finger that you take to pull that trigger, my God will have to give permission for those fingers to move. Besides, my God could stop the oxygen that you use to breathe, and you would drop dead like a chicken. So I'm not afraid of you."

The guy looked at me, lowered the gun, and said, "You have a lot of faith in your God. With that kind of faith, man, come on in."

As I entered the room I saw about eight men seated around a table, sniffing cocaine. I inquired about the young lady who then came out. We prayed together, and I encouraged her to continue coming to the meetings. That same night the same guy who had threatened me with the gun had a fight with her, and she pushed a knife straight through his heart, killing him on the spot. It was so unfortunate that he had to die that way. God promise that when we stand up for Him He will cause our enemy to fall at our feet. I was determined now more than ever to do His will because He had showed me in no uncertain terms that He could use me for His glory. I was ready to go anywhere and everywhere as a witness for Him. He had ordained me to be only a mouth piece for Him and I was ready and willing to go wherever He needed to send me.

A call came for us to go to Zambia, Africa, and as the plane landed, a red carpet led us straight to the VIP lounge. A motorcade led us to the Prime Minister's house, where we lived for the duration of the crusade. I smiled as I reflected on His promise that He would cause us to ride upon the high places. I could not believe that I was experiencing such kingly and royal treatment. God was about to break barriers down and set captives free. I was ready to be used by Him as a vessel of honor. The mountain top experience began as the meetings brought thousands of people to hear His word. God moved in a mysterious way and many miracles were performed.

The power of God moved mightily as we watched many demon-possessed claim their deliverance, and were set free from the evil hands of the enemy. On the night that we held the special prayer service for those who were bound by the spirit of evil, we saw the supernatural power from on high in full demonstration as the power oft the Holy Ghost took full control. An interesting account was that of a 17-year-old girl. After we prayed with her, she began to speak in deep, loud tones. Her eyes were like blood,, and she had the strength of about ten men. With that situation, the pastors gathered together to pray while seven of us remained, and we formed a chain around the young lady and prayed. She spoke again in the same deep voice, and one of the evangelists said, "Who are you?"

"We are legions, and we are many."

"We know, but in the name of Jesus Christ of Nazareth, come out of her!"

"Where should we go?"

The evangelist said, "Go to the mountains, for this is the property of the almighty God, and you have no right to possess that which is not yours." As he spoke those words, the girl began to shake and tremble as she sneezed, and then she exhaled and fell asleep.

When she awoke she said, "Where am I?"

The evangelist said, "Say thank you, Jesus."

She repeated, "Thank you Jesus. Where is my mother?" For the first time in a long time, mother and daughter were united, as she was delivered from the strong hold of the demons.

Many accepted the powerful message of salvation as they saw the demonstration of the Holy Spirit. The power of God moved and many wonders were performed. There was a young man who was sick unto death. His body was covered with raw sores from AIDS as he laid in the hospital and waited there to die. His family had seen the working of God's supernatural power and believed that the same God was able to deliver him from the aids virus. They asked that we pray for him, and the evangelistic team went to the hospital the next day but the authorities would not allow us in because the disease is highly contagious. The family decided to sneak him out of the hospital that night, through an open window on a stretcher, and brought him to the meeting.

Seeing the condition of the man's body, the evangelist said that we could not lay hands on him, but we would pray and ask the Holy Ghost to lay His hands upon him as we lifted him up in prayer. As we prayed, we could hear the man groaning in sheer agony. After what seemed to be only two minutes, the man sat up. By the time that the prayer was finished, the man stood up, so we prayed again, thanking God for his miraculous intervention in the life of his creation by the Holy Ghost.

We told the family to take the man back to the hospital and ask the doctors to do blood work on him. The family requested that a new set of blood work be done, but the doctors refused. One family member insisted that new blood work be done and offered to pay handsomely for the new tests. The tests were done, and the results came back negative. The puzzling result soon caused much questioning and other medical specialists were summoned to do a re- test, which also came back negative. The news was noised abroad and people were now coming from far and near. Many were convinced of the working of the power of God. , "for I am God, I wound and I heal, I kill and I make alive, I create and I destroy, for there is no other God beside me" (Deut 32:39).Thousands of souls accepted the message and many were healed of their illnesses. I was now empowered to be used even more by the divine Creator for I had seen His power hand at work, and the deliverance of his people. After the crusade I returned to Jamaica.

The hand of God continued to work with me as I returned home to Jamaica in 1990, as I answered the call once again in Kingston. One day as I was about to board the bus to do a visitation, I felt power of an unusual hand that and a familiar voice saying "Take a walk through the cemetery," I used the familiar shortcut and went to the home of an army sergeant to speak with his daughter. "Tell her not to keep her appointment this evening to coach the contestants for the annual beauty competition, but that she should go to the meetings tonight." The voice continued.

As I was heading in the direction of her home that Thursday evening, she was coming towards me. We stopped, facing each other in the middle of the cemetery. I told her what God had asked me to tell her, and she began to laugh, as I guess any normal person would do.

I said, "Will you change your mind and go with me this evening to the meeting?"

She became very angry and defensive and eventually walked away, leaving me standing in the middle of the cemetery. I watched her as she walked away, and then I said, "Father, I have done as you asked me to do."

That young woman, was determined to keep her appointment in St. Mary's that evening, and she left her home intending to reach her destination, but she never reached it. A search was made by the police and family members of her whereabouts. Thursday evening she did not show up, and Friday evening the contestants were very annoyed and concerned because they did not see her, knowing that Saturday evening was to be the show. And after an extensive search, her body was discovered on Sunday, naked and beheaded. This was a breaking point for me. But what troubled me the most was that on the very spot in the cemetery where we stood to deliver and receive the message of God, that young woman was buried. She was buried there, in the middle of the cemetery, where she will remain until the resurrection morning, "for we must all stand before the judgment seat of Christ to give an account of our lives on earth" (Rom 14:10).

I remained in Jamaica from 1990 until 1992, working in many crusades before leaving to answer a call in England. I watched the hand of God move mightily again and again. Many were brought into the fold. One night during the crusade I met a young woman who was trafficking drug for over 17 years. She came to the meeting and sat down at the back of the tent. She had been visiting a few nights but on this particular night I was led to pray for her. As I prayed she started to cry and I continued to pray for her deliverance. That night she gave her heart to the Lord and testified that there were nine of them in her group of friends and that 5 of them were killed and 2 were in jail and one was deported. She explained that God had saved her from death and she believed that He had brought her to the tent that night in particular for me to speak to her about her soul salvation. God is always willing use the vessel that makes itself available to be used by Him. I reflected on my past life and remember how God had indeed saved my life so many times. I remembered how I was completely locked in fear and He gave me the spirit of boldness. One of the most challenging experiences I had was with an Elderly lady's husband who wanted absolutely nothing to do with the bible. She had requested bible study, but wanted nothing to do with it. I prayed and asked God for wisdom to reach him somehow. I soon discovered that he loved to discuss politics and I decided to use that as a means to get to him.

One day as I went to study with his wife I was careful to wrap the bible in news paper and decided to read to him from the book of Daniel because he was quite knowledgeable of history and was able to recognize some of the very prophetic messages in Daniel 7. I continued to study with him from the book for over three weeks. He had no clue that I was using the very bible that he despised. I had now gotten him to a point where he was hooked and bought him his own bible. By this time he was convicted and converted and he and his wife were baptized into the message. I never fail to marvel at the handy work of God. He has His way of claiming His own.

I returned to Jamaica and continued to work for the cause of the Gospel. I was now working full time in crusades and was passionate about the work of the Lord. I was now convinced that He had called me for service and had a strong zeal to follow in his will regardless of what happens.

One morning around 5 o'clock I was awakened again by the Voice that I had learned to listen for. He told me to go and pray with a particular member of parliament.

I arrived at his office around 10 a.m., but could not see him until around 5 p.m. for he had been seeing people all day. I was the last person to see him that day, and as I walked into the office, he said, "How can I help you?"

"I am not here to ask you for help, sir."

"Then why are you here?"

"I was sent here by God to pray for you. You have been seeing and helping people all day, and God has taken note of that, and has sent me here to pray for you."

When I was through speaking to him, the tears began to stream down his face. He said, "Sir, will you come back another time?"

I got up to leave and he said, "Never mind, come and have a seat." Do you know what you have just said to me?"

"Yes," I replied.

He said, "I am also a member of a church, and a politician for so many years and not even my own pastor, or any pastor has ever offered to come and pray with me."

I said, "Sir, I did not know that, but God knew, and that is why He has sent me to pray for you."

The man cried and cried like a baby, and when he could speak, he asked, "What church do you attend?"

I told him, "The Adventist Church."

"I will visit your church with you this weekend," and true to his word, he drove 52 miles to meet me at church that Sabbath, inviting me afterwards to come to his office every Thursday to pray with him before he began the day's work. He was so grateful to God for sending me to minister to him that he offered to pay for my wife's tuition throughout college. He also set me up in business, which did not last very long, for that was not my calling. Very soon, I again left Jamaica to answer a call in New York.

I was soon involved in crusades since I had truly given myself for service. One day, a very old lady was attending the nightly meetings faithfully. It was my privilege and joy to visit her, and to help her make her decision for the Lord. As I arrived at her home, she was happy to see me. But when I asked her to make Jesus her choice and surrender for baptism, she told me that she was not yet ready.

"Not ready yet, ma'am!" I took a piece of paper and drew a straight line and a figure of a woman standing right on the brink. I said, "Ma'am, this is your sad condition, you are right on the threshold, and anything that come against you now will knock you right over the brink. And you're telling me you are not ready yet. Ma'am, when are you going to be ready?" I handed her the pledge card and a pencil, and I said, in as soft and loving a voice as I could, "Mother, sign the card for Jesus."

She did, and I prayed with her and committed her to the Lord. At baptism, she was the first person to go into the water, because she was ready.

During that same crusade, a young woman came to the meetings every night. She wanted to give her heart to Jesus and be baptized, but she was living as a common law wife with the father of her four children. She fought with him almost every night, but she did not know how to break away. I told her that I would come by to talk with him. But as early as we reached the house that morning, the man was still intoxicated from the night before. We left promising to return, but we did not go back for a while.

Then one morning, I was hard pressed to go and look for him. When I reached the home, he was there, sober, but asleep. She woke him up, and he came out into the yard to speak with us, joined by his lady. We stood under a cool coconut tree and I spoke with him, encouraging him to marry the young lady for the sake of her own salvation and the stability of the family, in rearing her children in a godly manner.

As I spoke with him, the Voice that usually speaks to me said, "Somers see that bunch of coconuts up in the tree? Ask him to give you one, and then move away from under the tree, all of you."

I said, "Brother, you see those coconuts? Give me one," and immediately the whole bunch was hacked off and fell down and burst all over the yard.

We were all amazed, and right there and then, the man began to tremble. When he could speak, he said, "Is it a sign that God is going to cut off my life?" I smiled to myself because I knew that this was the working of the Holy Spirit.

The following night He showed up at the service with the young lady at his side and they continued to attend all of the nightly meetings together. They were married and, together, as man and wife they were baptized and became free mortal agents in the church, for whom the Son sets free is free indeed (John 8:36).

The call of God later took me to Queens, New York, and once again, the awesome power of God Almighty manifested itself during a baptismal service. I was the evangelist responsible for preparing people for baptism. As I was waiting on a young man who was preparing to enter the baptistery, that Voice spoke to me again saying, "Somers, go outside the tent to the lady sitting inside the taxi and tell her to give me her heart today." And usually when I hear God speak once, I move immediately but this time I was caught up in the serenity of the moment, and did not move right away.

And in a very firm tone, that Voice spoke again, and I knew that I had offended the Most High. I said, "Lord, what should I say?"

He said, "Tell her that the I Am, that I Am said give me your heart today."

I dropped the cards that I was holding in my hand and ran out of the tent. I saw the lady sitting in the taxi, parked with the car windows partly up. I knocked on the glass and she rolled the glass down completely.

I said, "Ma'am, the I Am, that I Am, sent me to you to tell you that for 20 years I have been watching you and caring for you. But today, harden not your heart, give me your heart." I said, "Turn the car around and pull into the tent yard and give your heart to the Lord today."

She began to cry and said to me, "Sir you don't know this, but 20 years ago I was baptized in the Seventh Day Adventist Church, but I was mistreated and I left.

I said, "God is calling you today, He will take care of those who offend you."

While the evangelist was finishing the appeal, she made her way to the front. She said, "I did not come for baptism, I don't have any clothes to go into the water."

I asked, "Why were you outside then?"

She said, "I came to pick up my daughter."

I said, "Ma'am, God sent me to you today, don't disobey Him."

Then her daughter ran up to her, and both mother and daughter were baptized that day. I realized that not many people were familiar with the advent message. I considered myself a messenger from God who needed to show them the way. I realized that there were many blinded eyes that needed to be open, and many captives that needed to be set free. The task was great but the work had to be done. It dawned on me that there are even many spiritual leaders who are afraid to tell their congregation that The Seventh day Sabbath should be observed as demonstrated by Jesus Himself. Many of the crusades that I have been involved in unfolds the mystery to thousands of eager souls who never heard about the Adventist church and the observance of the Sabbath.

Breaking through

God is still calling His faithful children to enter His temple presence on His Holy Sabbath Day, according to the commandment. Six days shall thou labor and do all thy work, but the seventh day is still the Sabbath of the Lord, thy God. It is good to sing, this is the day that the Lord has made, because He has made them all, there is only one that He has blessed and set apart for holy use (Gen 2:1-3), and that which God has blessed no man can curse or change.

The very number seven is embodied in Jesus Christ, to move the hand of God on our behalf. And so, one Sabbath afternoon, our prayer group in New York gathered as a custom to thank God for His presence among us in the divine service. There were seven of us, and many wonderful works were wrought by the number seven, for it is God's sign, and seal (Ezek 20:12, 20) to His people. Walls were torn down by the number seven.

And so on the seventh day, Sabbath, God watches out for His children who are obedient to Him, to cushion the blow of adversity. And this was the experience one Sabbath as we gathered to pray and witnessed the power of God as He intervened in the family of one of our prayer warriors. There were seven of us, God's number, that perfect number that gets God's attention. I was in the middle of prayer when, suddenly God spoke to me in that Voice that I have come to know and love. I stopped and everybody raised their heads and asked what had happened.

I said, "Trouble is coming to your house," and pointed at a particular sister in the circle. I began to pray again on the sister's behalf. The Tuesday following, that sister's husband, the driver of a school bus, was involved in an accident that killed several passengers and broke his own neck as the bus overturned and dropped of a cliff. The Sister's husband was paralyzed from the neck down.

The Sister called me and said, "Brother Somers, you saw this coming. Please come and pray for my husband."

I said, "Yes, I will pray for him," and we went back to the same spot in the church where the revelation was given. I prayed, asking the Lord to reverse the situation. Three weeks later, that brother left the hospital. To this day, he has not been back for that injury.

"Is anything too hard for the Lord?"

Two years prior to this family crisis, this same sister's nephew met in an accident. He became paralyzed and was on life support for a while. One day as I visited him, her aunt, who was a psychic, challenged my God; the God who locked the lions' jaws. The One who made a road through the Red Sea and then closed the road again, for His people, who spoke in thunderous tones, and the earth shook, as He inscribed His holy law on tablets of stone, with His own finger. And even to this day, when God chooses to exercise His power through the elements of nature, who can stand before Him? Lightning that seem to split the skies asunder followed by deep loud claps of thunder send humanity into moments of fear and uncertainty.

And this agent of darkness challenged my God, Israel's God, The God, the God of Abraham, Isaac, and Jacob, that no god could make her nephew walk again. And any god who can do so she, the creature, will acknowledge him as God.

Well, there is nothing better my God loves than to hear a challenge from Beelzebub. So I knelt beside the bed of the young man, and said, "My Father, you have just heard Satan challenge you and your power to raise this young man up from this bed."

Many people, churchgoers, are bound in the churches today, shackled by some chain of circumstances that seem to overpower them, holding them hostage for a lifetime, because their connection with God is broken. Jesus empowered his disciples to go out and heal all manner of diseases, and sin is the biggest of them all. And the twelve returned, saying that even the demons were subject to us.

God wants to do the same for His church today. In fact, He has promised that in the last days we shall do greater works than He did, but sin will keep us shackled when we are disobedience. God is looking for a relationship with His people. Our heart will stay with Him. Yes, "Hearken unto Me, a righteous people in whose Heart is my Law" (Isa 51:7).

Chapter VI

Knocked Down But Not Out

I worked and labored in New York. My experience of how the Lord God had used me preceded me near and far. The evangelist with whom I served in Queens was anxious to have me on staff at his church, but this was not without a challenge. During that same period, another vacancy opened as a result of a dispute between the pastor and the Bible worker who was stationed at this particular church for over 17 years, whom the church members loved and grew so fondly of. The pastor of another church was not too keen about my zealous approach to evangelism and harbored some resistance to having me join his staff. He requested my qualifications, wanting to know whether I held a bachelor's degree, or otherwise.

The enemy already knew that he had knocked me unconscious as a child, tried to kill me, and succeeded in keeping from obtaining a good education. Now he was out to use this flaw against me. I said, "My work and experience have already been tested and tried, and that was the only qualifications I hold." I knew that God had always fought my battles for me and would continue to fight them. The pastor agreed to give me one month's probation, to see if I would win souls not for the glory of God, but for the glory of man.

I was placed on a three-week trial at the church, and in two weeks, God used me to win seven precious souls for the kingdom of heaven. These names were not only written on the church's book but inscribed in the Lamb's book of life, if they remain faithful to Jesus.

It all started on the first morning of my three-week trial, that Sabbath, as I held a Bible class. I saw a young man sitting attentively, and I said to him, "Why are you running away from God?"

He said, "How do you know that?"

"The Holy Ghost told me so."

He said, "I have attended, a number of nightly meetings at a crusade and every time the appeal was made, I got up and left."

I said, "I know, but next Sabbath is your day."

"My day for what?"

"To be married to Jesus in baptism," and that brother just could not contain the tears that flowed. Sure enough he was baptized among the seven.

Later on that same day, an older man walked into the Bible class. He did not have an invitation, and he had heard nothing about the church before. But as I was doing the Bible study, the Holy Ghost said to me, "Tell him, next week Sabbath, Jesus wants to be married to you. He has been waiting for you, has been keeping you for all these many years, and today you have heard His Voice. Harden not you heart and do not send Him not away with a broken heart over you."

On the following Sabbath, to mark the end of my first two weeks, the Holy Ghost did His work through me, and seven persons joined their Lord in baptism. I take credit for none of it; only a willing heart to do God's bidding for as long as I live.

After the baptism, the pastor called an emergency meeting to determine my future with the church, because I had only one more week to finish my three-week probation. Their opinion would decide my fate. But the church members had accepted me and were beginning to learn to love me, and unanimously they voted for me to remain on as the Bible worker on staff. I knew that God had his hand on my life and even though I was knocked down by different circumstances Christ was there to uphold me. I was never knocked out. His love is never failing and his grace has always been extended towards me. I know that despite the difficult times in life God has always had a purpose on my life.

I battled with the whole matter of not having a degree, but I know that when God calls you for service you are more than qualified. The church agreed to keep me, and I know that it was the hand of God on my life. The church decided to fight for me and sent a letter to the Conference requesting that I remain as the Bible worker, but this was again ignored and sent to the executive committee. Once again, my qualifications and resumé were called into question, and I stood my ground, that my work and experience preceded me. About 80 percent of the executive committee voted to employ me in January 2001. And in one year, without any big crusade or revival, the Holy Ghost worked on the hearts of men and women to harvest over 100 precious souls into the kingdom. I was convinced that when God fights your battles they are guaranteed victories. The members had grown fond of me and rejoiced at the Lord's success through me. I had given myself to service and I took my commitment seriously. God knew my heart and He never failed to remind me that His hand is on my life.

For over two years I worked at that church with tremendous success. The pastor was transferred to another church. He was replaced with a pastor that I had known from my teen years. I felt very good about this, and I looked forward to an amiable relationship with him, for he had been my youth pastor, but the half was yet to be told.

After the first two weeks, he asked me to produce my qualifications and resumé.

I told him that I did not see the need for it, because I was not seeking a job, and I did not see the relevance of requesting it now. Moreover, I was employed when he met me and when he took up the pastorate of the church. If he wanted me to produce a record of the work I was doing or an account of the baptisms, and the matter of the material used during the periods of evangelism, I would be more than willing to present them to him. But any record of my qualifications and experience should be at the Conference office, where he could was at liberty to obtain the information he needed.

He decided that if I did not present the documents, he would not be willing to work with me, and he would communicate this to the Conference. I was dismissed from him as insubordinate.

I was summoned a third time to present my qualifications, and my response was the same. This only angered him more, as he reported me to the Conference for which we both worked. I realized that only my God could vindicate me from these atrocities.

Sure enough, I received a call from the disciplinary committee to meet with the pastor so that the matter could be resolved. But my only hope was in the mercy of my Heavenly Father. I called on all the prayer warriors that I had been privileged to work with from as far away as the Virgin Islands, and all over New York. We joined together in a prayer vigil on my behalf.

When I arrived at the meeting, I was invited to sit in a seat already prepared for me, and I could appreciate what Jesus meant when he said, "He was led as a lamb before the slaughter." To my surprise, the chairman of the meeting was the pastor's friend, but the pastor was not there himself. I was asked to tell the committee why I was there and to explain myself.

I said, "I cannot do that, because it is not right or legal to speak against the pastor if he is not there to defend his case, and I would not do it."

from Florida and went back to work. I felt spiritually low and decided the following week to take a day off on my birthday and just spend time on meditating with the Lord, in prayer and fasting. I needed to get a spiritual enrichment from on high.

While at home, I received a call from another pastor friend from my teen years, who was preparing for a seminar. He wanted to know if I had any information that he could use. I told him I did and that I would come over and bring them to him. I was traveling in toward the east, and I saw a car pulling out to head west, but the driver made a U-turn, lost control, and ran right into my car, injuring my neck, knee, and back.

After the accident, I asked the pastor friend who had asked for my help to assist me by taking me to the Conference office to report the accident and take copies of the police and medical reports. I was placed on disability for six months, suffering from cervical and lumbar radiculopathy, and I was put on bed rest. I continued with treatment after the six months and turned the legal aspects over to my lawyer, who inquired in writing whether I would be paid for as long as I was disabled. The answer was given in writing in the affirmative.

During that time I sought the face of God to inquire of Him the plan that He had for my life. I felt broken and wounded, lonely and rejected. No one came to see me .After the six- month period was over, I received a call asking me when I was returning to work. I told the caller that I was still having treatment and that the nature of my job required excessive walking and the climbing of stairs. There was no way that I could return to work at that time. I continued to receive my wages, which I thought was as a result of what the lawyer had investigated. I received another call from the Conference informing me that either I returned to work or I would be replaced. I replied that I was still experiencing much pain just by standing and that if I had to decide between the job and my health that my health would have to comes first. By the following week, I was replaced.

I was completely broken but I knew that God was trying to tell me something. Sometimes He closes one door to open another. I knew I needed to sit tight because He was only preparing me for greater service. A few months later I received a letter from the treasurer of the Conference asking me to return the moneys that I had received because I had not returned to work or they would take legal action to recover the funds. I called the treasurer and after discussing the matter with him, I asked him, "How could they write one thing to my lawyer, and request another from me?"

I had never received, a letter telling me that I was dismissed and I had not submitted a letter of resignation, so as far as I was concerned. I was being paid for disability according to the agreement made with my lawyer. The treasurer, promised to get back to me, but that did not happen. I called my pastor friend whom I was assisting when I got in the accident, to share the details of the matter with him. But he turned against me, and told me a brother to me. He agreed to take me to the embassy in his very old car. The morning that my wife and I set off for the embassy, in my cousin's very old car, the car broke down three times on the way, and I missed my 8 o'clock appointment.

The embassy operates from 8 o'clock a.m. to 10 o'clock a.m. I reached there at 11:45 a.m., and my wife was still laughing. The gate was closed, so my cousin said, "Maybe you should come back another day."

I said, "God said He was sending me, and I believe Him. So, I am going to knock on the door." A security guard opened the door just sufficiently enough to ask, "How can I help you?"

I said, "Sir, if you would open the door, I want to explain something to you."

He said, "Alright," and he opened the door.

I said, "I had an appointment for 8:30, but the car broke down three times, and that is why I am so late."

He said to one of his junior officers, "Come and get this key and take this gentleman and his wife around through the gate, and bring the keys back to me."

When we got inside, there was a line of about 300 people. And oh what weeping, as people were turned down! But the security officer took me straight to the front of the line, in the front of all those people. He led me to a counter to a woman, the very same woman that was shown to me in the dream.

She looked at me searchingly and said, "The only reason that I am giving you this visa is because I can see you are a man of God." She took my passport, still searching me over, and said, "Who is that behind you?"

I said, "My wife."

"Do you want to take her with you?"

"Yes, ma'am."

"Give me her passport as well. Wait here for a few minutes."

I waited for what seemed only a few minutes. She stamped our passports and handed them back to me. "The Lord is with you. Go and do His bidding."

"Thank you, ma'am." I said, and left with eagerness to do His will.

When I reached New York, I met a man whom I had known only by praying with him on the phone, through our partners in a prayer chain. But then I had the opportunity and privilege of meeting him face to face, and what a happy meeting it was.

After he greeted me, he took out his checkbook and wrote me a check for 10,000 dollars to help me get settled in. Then he asked, "Do you want to work with my church?"

I said, "I would like to, but I don't think I can do that unless your church is in greater New York, for that is where I was sent." And I showed him a quote that was given to me in the dream, from a well-known author of the Church on "Evangelism" pages 384-385 by Ellen G. White.

The Work in the Large American Cities (New York)

"The Message to Go – While in New York in the winter of 1901, I received light in regard to the work in that great city. Night after night the course that our brethren should pursue passed before me. In Greater New York the message is to go forth as a lamp that burneth. God will raise up laborers for this work, and His angels will go before them...."

"...Working After God's Order, not according to man's devising"

He smiled and said, "That is my church, in Greater New York City." He further explained that his church had not had a baptism for three and a half years, and they had been praying to God to please send someone to help them. And here you are."

I stayed with that church, and in three months, without any big crusade or revival, 14 people were baptized. All these experiences were coming back to me. I could not understand the course my life was taking and so I decided to play back the chords of all my experiences. Where did I go wrong? What did I do? The answers did not come and I continued to reflect on my previous paths of the journey.

Chapter VIII

God's Timing

I reflected on the time I was holding a seven-day series of prayer and fasting meeting, and one night as I went to bed, I had a dream that a man came to me and told me that he was going to make me sick so that I could be admitted to the hospital because he had a work for me to do on the wards, but that I should not be afraid. I was afraid and turned my head, but by the time I looked back to ask him what kind of sickness it would be, he was gone. I got up the following morning and packed my bag and told my mother that I was going to be admitted to the hospital, but that she should not worry when she didn't see me come home that evening.

The following day as I was praying, I began to feel very ill. As time went by, I became so extremely ill that I had to go and see my doctor. His diagnosis was that I be sent immediately to the hospital, because my blood pressure had gone beyond that of human ability to cope or exist. He called the ambulance for me, but when it came I had left to go on an appointment because I had to pray for a family. When I was finished, I told the family that I was going to be admitted into a hospital. The wife looked at me as if I had gone berserk and out of my mind

On reaching the hospital, the medical staff was on the alert, having already inquired of my doctor, on several occasions, as to my whereabouts. I was examined, and immediately prepped with life support, because they said that they had found some complications and only time would tell whether they had to do surgery. I was put to bed. That night, one of the men lying beside me died, and it put all of the patients in a somber mood, fearful and uncertain whether any one of them would be next. I got up that morning and asked the medical staff if I could hold a devotional service to minister to the patients, and permission was given. And that was the beginning of my ministry for the seven days that I spent on the ward. At 6 o'clock every morning I was up and went from bed to bed throughout the ward, praying for the sick and laying hands upon them. The nurses and doctors looked forward every morning for the prayers, saying that the patients were more controlled and manageable as a result of the devotions.

After three days my blood pressure was back to normal, and there were no further signs of any complications. But the medical team decided to hold me on the ward for 7 days before discharging me. When I was discharged three other patients were also discharged; and those men continued to ask for Bible studies. Three Sabbaths afterwards, they were baptized. The doctors gave me permission to continue the devotions at the hospital until God sent me to Greater New York.

I could not help but reflect on all the experiences that I had and the revelation of the power of the most High that was manifested and now it was all gone. It was all taken away. I raised my thoughts and reminisced on the powerful ways in which God had used me to touch the lives of individuals who needed someone to show them the way. I then concluded that Greater New York was not my final destination, it was only my rest stop.

Chapter IX

Speak and I Will Answer

My mind started to wonder back on the ministries I had where God was able to speak to me and use me for His glory. The experience of what happened one Sabbath gave me the push to go on. I was about to preach, I began to pray. But I felt haunted by the spirit of evil. So I stopped praying and said openly, "Somebody here is under attack." And then I said, "In the name of Jesus, release that soul!"

Suddenly a young woman got up and rushed out of the church, knocking down everybody in her path. I went out of the church to where she lay on the ground and called her by name and said, "what happened?"

A voice responded in a deep angry tone, "I am not Racquel."

I said,"Yes, you are Racquel."

The voice said,"Don't call me Racquel."

So I said, "Hey Satan, who are you talking to like that? I am a servant of the Most High God. Don't you raise your voice at me."

"Ok, ok."

I said, "It is not ok, because we are not any kind of friends. Don't ever talk to me like that again."

She sat up and her mother came to her, but she would not allow anybody to touch her or speak to her except me. She did everything that I asked, but there was a chain around her neck with a pendant of three fingers. And these three prong-like fingers began to wiggle, frightening all who looked on. So I asked her mother to remove the chain so that I could pray, but she refused, saying that it was for her protection. I said, "I see why she is like that, and I cannot pray for her with the evil hanging around her neck."

So an aunt removed the chain, and I prayed, saying, "In the name of Jesus, get out of her," and immediately as she was sitting up, she fell to the ground, frothing from the mouth, and rolling over her eyes. Then she became very quiet and calm.

The demonic spirits lingered because she refused to give up her chain with the three-prong pendant. Eventually, her husband was called to take her to the hospital. But when he came, she refused to go into the car until I said, "Get into the car."

She said, "Ok, ok," so I rode with her to the hospital. Each time she attempted to do something funny, she would look behind at me and remain quiet. When we arrived at the hospital, the doctor could not touch her. She became very angry and overturned everything in the room, so the doctor ran out of the office.

I went into her room and said, "You listen to the doctor, and do as he says."

She said, "Ok, ok." And she did as the doctor asked. The doctor was able to administer some drugs to her that put her to sleep. Even demons and devils are subjected to the power of God. I realized that what God can do is certainly no secret.

Chapter X

Yours for Keeps

I had to rededicate my life for service. I was not sure where He wanted me to begin but I made a commitment with Him that I was His for keeps. God had already shown me that if I humble myself He would use me mightily. That was all I wanted. That was all I longed for. I said yes to His will and command and I was not about to give that up. I was willing to go wherever He wanted me to go.

In fact, He has said in these last days we shall do greater works than He has done, but sin will keep us shackled, for all disobedience is sin. God is looking for a relationship with His people, for when there is a love relationship, not only will the mouth confess Him (Isa 29:13), but the heart will obey Him. Yes, "Hearken unto Me a righteous people in whose Heart is my Law" (Isa 51:7). And this revelation was made clear to me in a dream the Lord gave unto me in July, 2006.

One night as I slept, I dreamt that I was walking toward a little church. The closer I got to it, the louder I heard a confused noise that was coming from what appeared to be a meeting of some sort from within the church. The closer I got, the louder the noise grew, until suddenly, a bright light appeared in the sky over the church. In that light was what seemed to be a head with a glittering golden crown, with many little crowns upon it. I tried to look at it, but it was so bright that I was blinded, so I buried my head in the earth. Then there was a voice like thunder that cried out, "My church! My church! My heart is broken over my church. Broken, broken, broken."

I tried to look up, but the light was so bright and intense that I could not see. I heard the echo of the word broken as it faded into a stillness. Then I got up and looked to see if there was anybody else around, and I saw a man coming towards me. Before I could speak, he asked, "Did you hear that voice? It said, `My church! My church! My church! Oh, my heart is broken over my Church."

And I said, "Thank God you heard it," and suddenly the man disappeared, and I was left alone. I awoke, crying and shaking so terribly, feeling my flesh to see it was real, because I thought Judgment had come to the world. I was very scared, numb, and very sullen, but I wanted to know the meaning of the dream. Then I realized that I still had a work to do to warn people of the great and terrible day of the Lord (Zeph 1:4-18).

Work to do, but how was I to accomplish this, when I was still shackled by oppression and opposition? For God had led me through thorny paths to Florida after completing through me His work in the great metropolitan cities of New York, for in the quotation that was initially given to me in the dream from the book, *Evangelism*, pages 384-385, it spoke of New York and the larger cities of America:

"The Lord calls upon those who have gained an experience in the Cause to take up and carry forth in its spheres the work to be done, wherever it is needed, even the larger Cities of America."

And so my work was not peculiar only to New York, but throughout the world, wherever the Lord was pleased to lead me. Nevertheless, I was torn by unemployment and forced into a divorce that I hated and despised; separating me from my family. This devastated me immensely. But then I remembered 2 Cor 4:7-10. I was determined that though persecuted, I was not forsaken, cast down but not destroyed. And I realized that the enemy was not finished with me yet as He tried to break every part of my will to survive. But I was determined to fight and with God's help to break through the shackles that so long took control of my life. His strength is perfect even in our weaknesses and through Jesus Christ my Lord I knew I had to be the victor.

I decided that I needed to start all over again. God had not given me a spirit of fear and I was going to move in accordance with His will. Faced with no job, I traveled to Lakeland, Florida and joined one of the little churches in that community, as I sought employment with them. Initially, I was invited to join them for a seven-week evangelist campaign in August, 2006, and was asked to work along with a team of Bible counselors. But once again the rod of injustice prevailed against me, for I was not paid for my services. Once again I found it very difficult and frustrating to provide for myself and my family.

At the end of the evangelistic campaign, I began to search for employment outside of the church. But everywhere I turned, the barriers went up and the obstacle of freedom to witness and worship drove me into a quandary of a spiritual alliance. I was brought back to consciousness when one of the Bible counselors with whom I was assigned to work for those seven weeks at the church, reminded me of who I am, and whose I am.

She asked me a penetrating question that awakened my spiritual awareness of why I was in the United States. "How can you leave the work of God to go and serve tables? Do you not know that He who puts in his hand to the plow and turns back will be destroyed?"

"What should I do then, I must survive."

"Go back to God, and ask Him. I can't tell you what to do, but I know that the God I know and serve will never throw away or fire His servants unless they give Him just cause to do so. So you need to work it out with Him. He is the one who appointed you. I promise that I will help you in any way that I can."

I thought about her remarks, and with much prayer and searching, I soon realized that I had been given a mandate to carry on with the work. Immediately a little light began to shine upon my path.

My very good friend and pastoral colleague whom I knew from my youth were living in New York, and I had been privileged to work with Him there. But as the Lord had ordained it, he and his family relocated to Florida. The opportunity came and I embraced it as I sought his help and assistance as my spiritual tutor and friend in spreading the gospel of the soon coming of Jesus to the community of Lakeland.

So on January 6, 2007, God began a ministry of reconciliation under the leadership of this pastor and his family, with whom I now serve as the associate pastor. I went in search of a building because we needed to find a place of our own to worship, and the vision that we had, necessitated a much bigger place because we expected to see bigger things happening. I heard about a building and discovered that it was available for our use. I did not know where to find the owners so I went from door to door until the person was found. This was one of the greatest workings of God that we saw. Week after week we would see new faces as they joined us in worship and remained with us. The membership moved from 7 to over 40 and God has been adding to this little fledging group daily. After much searching and disappointment, God has provided this great church, complete with all the amenities and seating facilities conducive for worship, for just a monthly donation toward the maintenance and upkeep of the property. My God is an awesome God, who knows how to show Himself in favor of those who trust and depend upon Him.

One of the high points of my childlike faith that proves God is with us in this work, is the free gift of a church building and its real estate, which was given to the little group to worship in. It has a seating capacity for over 300 persons, with carpeted floor and padded chairs, and a very large fellowship hall complete with tables and chairs, and an equally large furnished kitchen with a two large four-burner stoves. All from the hand of a God who knows the way in less than six months of the birth of the new Maranatha Adventist Church, in Lakeland, Florida..

I have been set free from the shackles of poverty for I now live in a beautiful home with my family. God has provided a loving and caring wife and my mom no longer has to worry about life's maintenance. I broke through the shackles that held me as a caged bird and I am now in partnership with the God of the universe in ministry. If I remain humble and faithful God will fill that church with not only 300 people but I have a vision that He is going to break down more barriers, unshackle those who are bound, and He is going to use that church as a lighthouse in Polk County, Florida.

The church has already seen many miracles. People have been healed from grave illnesses. God has restored broken homes and many have recognized that His presence is with us. God has blessed the church as it now serves the community. A program for community service was also implemented to help our needed children to progress academically in math and reading. We know that soon we will be able to extend the program to offer greater services because it is God's work and God's church and no man can stand in the way of the Lord.

Every Sabbath not only the spiritual man is fed but the physical. It is a wonder what God has done. I am still traveling on Hallelujah Boulevard because I have been redeemed. I have broken through the shackles that held my life as a captive to sin. My life and ministry is now a blessing. There is no need for us to question God's doing because He holds the keys to our lives. We need to put him to the test and prove him because He will never fail. But God has always sustained me, and when I had to go through the difficulties of servanthood, I was encouraged by three special songs that consoled me with their messages.

"If He carried the weight of the world upon His shoulders, then I know my brother, my sister that He can carry me." ("He Will Carry You")

"A song writer wrote "For the God of the Mountain is still God of the Valley, and when things go wrong, He will make them right."

"So I found my peace, real peace in knowing and serving Him as my Lord and dearest friend." You too can find the peace that passes all understanding. If you get to know him not just as a Savior but also as a friend, your life will never be the same because He will break every fetters of sin, sickness discouragement, and unhappiness He will break through the shackles that dominate your life. He can break through for you as He did for me.

References

Brown, Scott Wesley. "He Will Carry You." Copyright 1982 Birdwing Music/Cherry Lane Music Publishing Co., Inc.

Printed in the United States
153416LV00001B/2/P